GOD
IN STORY

THE GATHERING PLACE SERIES
A project guided by Daryl L. Smith

The Gathering Place: a series of books for people interested in exploring faith issues in a non-threatening setting. Each book uses questions, Bible selections, discussion, and group service as means for this exploration.

Don•Q•Dox: a resource-creation label of The Orlando Fellowship—
an incarnational, missional-ministry community.
Don•Q—The fictional knight *Don Quixote* (Miguel de Cervantes, 1605), whose most famous adventure includes meeting the tavern prostitute Aldonza and calling her to become the beautiful Dulcinea.
•Dox—Documents/tools/vehicles for discovery.

As the name implies, we are on a quest to discover life as it was meant to be and invite others to join that quest. We believe that God's image is planted deeply within each of us, but most times we cannot hear the call of the "impossible dream" without the company of others who can see in us things we don't see in ourselves.

GOD IN STORY

An 8-week Guide for Discussion and Service Groups

Brian Babcock, Patricia Clarke, Carolyn Smith and James Sullivan

RESOURCE *Publications* • Eugene, Oregon

GOD IN STORY
An 8-week Guide for Disussion and Service Groups

Copyright © 2013 Brian Babcock, Patricia Clarke, Carolyn Smith, and James Sullivan. All rights reserved. Except for brief quotations in critical publications or reviews, no part of this book may be reproduced in any manner without prior written permission from the publisher. Write: Permissions, Wipf and Stock Publishers, 199 W. 8th Ave., Suite 3, Eugene, OR 97401.

Scripture quotations mared MSG are taken from *The Message*, copyright © 1993, 1994, 1995, 1996, 2000, 2001, 2002. Used by permission of NavPress Publishing Group. All rights reserved.

Scripture quotations marked NIV are taken from the HOLY BIBLE, NEW INTERNATIONAL VERSION®. Copyright © 1973, 1978, 1984 Biblica. Used by permission of Zondervan. All rights reserved.

Resource Publications
An Imprint of Wipf and Stock Publishers
199 W. 8th Ave., Suite 3
Eugene, OR 97401
www.wipfandstock.com

ISBN 13: 978-1-62032-931-3

Manufactured in the U.S.A.

Interior Design: Carolyn B. Smith

Special thanks to **Beth Burton, Wendelyn Perceful, Octavius Smith** and **Luis Soto,** who were members of CD511 The Pastor and Christian Discipleship at Asbury Theological Seminary—Florida, January 2012.
Thanks also to **Brian Russell** for his scholarly guidance.

GOD IN STORY

CONTENTS

Why This Book? 1

Session 1: Something from Nothing? 3
(Genesis 1:1–31; 2:1–3)

Session 2: Sex Plus?... 10
(Genesis 2:18–25; 3:1–20))

Session 3: Why Do People Act That Way?.. 17
(Genesis 16:1–16; 21:9–21)

Session 4: Who's Got Your Back? 23
(Genesis 45:1–19)

Session 5: Have I Gone Nuts? 29
(1 Samuel 25:1–34)

Session 6: Are You Kidding Me? 35
(Jonah 3; 4)

Session 7: How Will We Make It? 40
(Ruth 1:1–22; 2:19–23; 4:13–17)

Session 8: Who Has the Map? 47
(Exodus 3:1–12)

We Serve Together 52

Group Leader Notes 54

Why This Book?

Christians believe in God, too!

The original term "Christian" was simply an ancient name given to people who radically followed Jesus. In their language (Greek) the word means "Christ's-ones"—"Christ" referring to Jesus as the Jewish Messiah (or "sent one").

Unfortunately, Christianity became a world religion; a religion that frequently hasn't looked much like Jesus. Over the centuries, many who called themselves Christian have based their beliefs on their own cultural, social, or political systems—rather than on him. Yet, Christianity has also always included authentic Jesus-followers from all nationalities, ethnicities, and languages.

That said, it's true that most Christians talk more about Jesus than God. Yet, one of the primary beliefs of Jesus-followers is that there is one God made up of three individual, equal beings, existing together—the Source of everything. Obviously, that's a complicated concept. But to our best understanding of the Bible we see the three persons who make up God described with the names:
God,
Jesus,
The Holy Spirit.

In the Old Testament (the first part of the Christian Bible and the majority of Jewish sacred writings), God (called Creator, King, Sustainer, among other names) is described as the primary person of God who interacts with humans.

The New Testament (the second part of the Christian Bible) tells the story of God coming to earth as the God-human, Jesus (the baby celebrated at Christmas). Jesus-followers believe that Jesus walked on Earth for about 33 years before he was killed (crucified for his living and teaching), then he came back to life after three days (his resurrection celebrated at Easter), before leaving Earth to go back to "heaven."

The Holy Spirit, also referred to in the New Testament, is the God-person who came to Earth as God's presence in the lives of all who believe in and follow Jesus—to help Jesus-followers actually live like him.

So, whether you've ever been to church, read the Bible, or know about Jesus, you've probably had thoughts about God. Maybe you've wondered whether God exists or what God is like. We get to know others through personal experience, what others say about them, or what people say about themselves. The same is true with God.

So, this book looks at a few stories in the Old Testament to help us catch a glimpse this God—and how God interacted with humans from the moment life began until Jesus came on the earthly scene.

TO THE GROUP LEADER:

Welcome to a different kind of Bible discussion resource. This isn't about learning facts or memorizing verses. It's about studying the Bible in community (where learning works best). This study is created to connect three stories: your story, God's story and my story. Lives are transformed at that juncture.

Each session concludes with directions to help group attendees move into service—**another unique feature of this study**. Every healthy group will include study, group-member care and mission (serving others who are not group members).

Please take time to read through the "Group Leader Notes" at the back (p. 58), where you'll find important ideas for your role as group leader. You will facilitate and guide during the coming weeks. Also, look over the "We Serve Together" ideas in the back of the book. Begin introducing the plan to serve together at the very first session.

1: Something from Nothing?

💡 THE BIG IDEA

Genesis is a book of beginnings—many very good beginnings. Some have argued about the length of the days described in this first chapter. Others have tried to make the book speak to scientific understandings, using it to guess the age of Earth. However, none of that is the author's pur-pose. That's like trying to study sailing by admiring a brilliant oil-painting of a ship at sea. Instead, the author has a higher purpose. She or he created a wonderful poem to point us toward the One who created all things; the One who is the source of everything living. So when the word "day" shows up, it's not the 24-hour day we would think of. It stands for a period of time when God's creative touch was bringing **newness out of nothingness**. The author wants us to know that the Eternal One was integrally involved in every aspect of creation, up to the final "project"—the creation of humans whom God declares, "so very good."

OPEN:
1. As you think back to your childhood, what is the best "project" you ever created? What, in your mind, made it best?

READ AND APPLY: Genesis 1:1–31 (MSG)

1-2First this: God created the Heavens and Earth—all you see, all you don't see. Earth was a soup of nothingness, a bottomless emptiness, an inky blackness. God's Spirit brooded like a bird above the watery abyss.

3-5 God spoke: "Light!" And light appeared.
  God saw that light was good
    and separated light from dark.

3

God named the light Day,
  he named the dark Night.
It was evening, it was morning—
Day One.

⁶⁻⁸ God spoke: "Sky! In the middle of the waters;
  separate water from water!"
God made sky.
He separated the water under sky
  from the water above sky.
And there it was:
  he named sky the Heavens;
It was evening, it was morning—
Day Two.

⁹⁻¹⁰ God spoke: "Separate!
  Water-beneath-Heaven, gather into one place;
Land, appear!"
  And there it was.
God named the land Earth.
  He named the pooled water Ocean.
God saw that it was good.

¹¹⁻¹³ God spoke: "Earth, green up! Grow all varieties
  of seed-bearing plants,
Every sort of fruit-bearing tree."
  And there it was.
Earth produced green seed-bearing plants,
  all varieties,
And fruit-bearing trees of all sorts.
  God saw that it was good.
It was evening, it was morning—
Day Three.

¹⁴⁻¹⁵ God spoke: "Lights! Come out!
  Shine in Heaven's sky!
Separate Day from Night.
  Mark seasons and days and years,

Lights in Heaven's sky to give light to Earth."
And there it was.

16-19 God made two big lights, the larger
to take charge of Day,
The smaller to be in charge of Night;
and he made the stars.
God placed them in the heavenly sky
to light up Earth
And oversee Day and Night,
to separate light and dark.
God saw that it was good.
It was evening, it was morning—
Day Four.

20-23 God spoke: "Swarm, Ocean, with fish and all sea life!
Birds, fly through the sky over Earth!"
God created the huge whales,
all the swarm of life in the waters,
And every kind and species of flying birds.
God saw that it was good.
God blessed them: "Prosper! Reproduce! Fill Ocean!
Birds, reproduce on Earth!"
It was evening, it was morning—
Day Five.

24-25 God spoke: "Earth, generate life! Every sort and kind:
cattle and reptiles and wild animals—all kinds."
And there it was:
wild animals of every kind,
Cattle of all kinds, every sort of reptile and bug.
God saw that it was good.

26-28 God spoke: "Let us make human beings in our image, make them
reflecting our nature
So they can be responsible for the fish in the sea,
the birds in the air, the cattle,
And, yes, Earth itself,
and every animal that moves on the face of Earth."

God created human beings;
  he created them godlike,
Reflecting God's nature.
  He created them male and female.
God blessed them:
  "Prosper! Reproduce! Fill Earth! Take charge!
Be responsible for fish in the sea and birds in the air,
  for every living thing that moves on the face of Earth."

²⁹⁻³⁰ Then God said, "I've given you
  every sort of seed-bearing plant on Earth
And every kind of fruit-bearing tree,
  given them to you for food.
To all animals and all birds,
  everything that moves and breathes,
I give whatever grows out of the ground for food."
  And there it was.

³¹ God looked over everything he had made;
  it was so good, so very good!
It was evening, it was morning—
Day Six.

Note: The original language (Hebrew) word for human— "adam," meaning "creature of the earth"— refers to both woman and man together, not "male."

---

2. If you had been hovering in the darkness, watching creation happen, which day would you have wanted to help with?

3. As you look at the days of creation, what do you notice about the order of what is created?

   What might the author have wanted us to know about God from the creation description?

4. In verses 26–28, it appears as if God has a discussion among its beings, to decide to make humans that carry the image or nature of God.

   Which part of this human creation story is a new insight to you?
   a. Both man and woman carry the nature of God.
   b. Humans were created last in the order.
   c. I don't really have any idea what this means.
   d. God stopped to talk about this part of creation when there didn't seem to be any discussion in the earlier days.
   e. Other _____

In Genesis 2:1–3 we have a sort of summary statement and a strange twist—God rested. Was God really tired? Or could it be that God has something else in mind? Let's read on ….

READ: Genesis 2:1–3 (MSG)

Heaven and Earth were finished, down to the last detail.

$^{2-4}$ By the seventh day
   God had finished his work.
On the seventh day
   he rested from all his work.
God blessed the seventh day.
   He made it a Holy Day
Because on that day he rested from his work,
   all the creating God had done.

This is the story of how it all started,
   of Heaven and Earth when they were created.

5. Try to imagine what God was thinking. Why do you think this part of the story is included? If God is really creator of all that exists, what's the deal about resting?
   a. Creating the universe takes a lot of energy.
   b. A good day off can clear the mind.
   c. God wanted humans to see a pattern for living.
   d. I cannot imagine why God rested.
   e. Other _____

6. We are told that God "blessed and made the seventh day holy." What might "resting," "blessing," and "making holy" have in common? Or do they have anything in common?

   If you were going to make a day holy, how would you do it?

7. When you consider the creation story, how might your thinking about Earth and nature be impacted or changed?

   How might your thinking about God be impacted or changed?

8. If you could have coffee with God, after reading this creation poem, what would be the most important question you'd ask?

   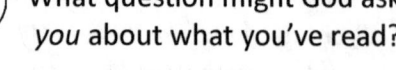 What question might God ask *you* about what you've read?

ACCOUNTABLE COMMUNITY:

9. What response do you think you should make after reading and discussing this part of God's story?

10. How would you want this group to affirm you this week? What might they do, so you sense their help?

WE SERVE:

11. What creative activity will you do this week—something that reminds you of how God wants us to care for the world? In nature, with animals, with humans?

_____
_____
_____
_____

WE PRAY:

The group leader closes the meeting with prayer.

2: SEX PLUS?

💡 THE BIG IDEA

In this reading, the author expands on the description of human creation that was announced in the poem of Genesis, chapter 1. You may remember that God decided to create humans in (or to carry) God's image. That's a huge thought, isn't it?

In chapter 2, the details of human creation are expanded. God takes some dirt, forms a single human (no gender at this point), breathes life into it, drops it down into a "magical" garden home, defines what it can and cannot eat, and gives it work to do. The human's first job is to name all the living creatures. In that process, the human discovers that it has no match. That's the signal. It's time for God to complete the human-creation task. The human is not complete—can never experience deep, God-planned relationships—without an equal partner. So God surgically split the human into a woman and a man—two persons who not only fit together sexually but also form a partner-relationship designed for oneness.

OPEN:
1. When was the first time you noticed that a person of the opposite gender was paying attention to you and you liked it? How old were you? How did you respond?

READ AND APPLY: Genesis 2:18–25 (NIV)

18 The LORD God said, "It is not good for the man to be alone. I will make a helper suitable for him."

¹⁹ Now the LORD God had formed out of the ground all the wild animals and all the birds in the sky. He brought them to the man to see what he would name them; and whatever the man called each living creature, that was its name. ²⁰ So the man gave names to all the livestock, the birds in the sky and all the wild animals.

But for Adam no suitable helper was found. ²¹ So the LORD God caused the man to fall into a deep sleep; and while he was sleeping, he took one of the man's ribs and then closed up the place with flesh.

²² Then the LORD God made a woman from the rib he had taken out of the man, and he brought her to the man.

²³ The man said,
 "This is now bone of my bones
  and flesh of my flesh;
 she shall be called 'woman,'
  for she was taken out of man."

²⁴ That is why a man leaves his father and mother and is united to his wife, and they become one flesh.

²⁵ Adam and his wife were both naked, and they felt no shame.

Notes: (1) The Hebrew word for "helper" (vs. 18) does not mean a weaker being. It's the same word used for God several times in the Old Testament. Instead, it means "someone greater because I really need help," or at least "an equal, standing face-to-face with me."
(2) The Hebrew word often translated "rib" (v. 20–21) is more accurately translated "side." So, out of the side of the single human, God formed a woman, then a man.

2. One aspect of "God's image" that's planted in all humans is the desire for deep relationship. What kinds of relationships seem most important from the creation story? Why?
    a. Between the first man and woman.
    b. Between all humans.
    c. Between humans and God.
    d. Between humans and all creation.
    e. All of the above.
    f. Other _____

3. Why do you think the author included the fact that the man and woman were not embarrassed of being naked?
   a. No one but God was around to notice.
   b. There was no need to be embarrassed in this shame-free paradise.
   c. Sexuality is God's very good idea, so celebrate.
   d. Total openness was possible before things "went bad."
   e. Other _____

In chapter 3 the scene changes as the couple decides to ignore God's directive. The result is broken relationship with God and broken relations between the humans. In verse 20 we hit the bottom of the pit. The male took for himself the Hebrew name *adam* (God's name for them together), named his wife (naming shows ownership, as with the animals), chose the name Eve (mother of all living) to show her value now came from birthing babies—a functionary role.

From their wondrous "naked and unashamed" relationship the humans drop into shame, fear, abuse, and brokenness.

Fortunately, this is not the end of the biblical story—but it does launch humanity into centuries of dark days before help comes to offer us a way back home.

READ: Genesis 3:1–20 (NIV)

Now the serpent was more crafty than any of the wild animals the LORD God had made. He said to the woman, "Did God really say, 'You must not eat from any tree in the garden'?"

² The woman said to the serpent, "We may eat fruit from the trees in the garden, ³ but God did say, 'You must not eat fruit from the tree that is in the middle of the garden, and you must not touch it, or you will die.'"

⁴ "You will not certainly die," the serpent said to the woman. ⁵ "For God knows that when you eat from it your eyes will be opened, and you will be like God, knowing good and evil."

⁶ When the woman saw that the fruit of the tree was good for food and pleasing to the eye, and also desirable for gaining wisdom, she took some and ate it. She also gave some to her husband, who was with her, and he ate it. ⁷ Then the eyes of both of them were opened, and they realized they were naked; so they sewed fig leaves together and made coverings for themselves.

⁸ Then the man and his wife heard the sound of the LORD God as he was walking in the garden in the cool of the day, and they hid from the LORD God among the trees of the garden. ⁹ But the LORD God called to the man, "Where are you?"

¹⁰ He answered, "I heard you in the garden, and I was afraid because I was naked; so I hid."

¹¹ And he said, "Who told you that you were naked? Have you eaten from the tree that I commanded you not to eat from?"

¹² The man said, "The woman you put here with me—she gave me some fruit from the tree, and I ate it."

¹³ Then the LORD God said to the woman, "What is this you have done?"
The woman said, "The serpent deceived me, and I ate."

¹⁴ So the LORD God said to the serpent,
"Because you have done this,
   "Cursed are you above all livestock
   and all wild animals!
You will crawl on your belly
   and you will eat dust
   all the days of your life.
¹⁵ And I will put enmity
   between you and the woman,
   and between your offspring and hers;
he will crush your head,
   and you will strike his heel."

¹⁶ *To the woman he said,*
  "I will make your pains in childbearing very severe;
  with painful labor you will give birth to children.
Your desire will be for your husband,
  and he will rule over you."

¹⁷ *To Adam he said, "Because you listened to your wife and ate fruit from the tree about which I commanded you, 'You must not eat from it,'*
  "Cursed is the ground because of you;
  through painful toil you will eat food from it
  all the days of your life.
¹⁸ *It will produce thorns and thistles for you,*
  and you will eat the plants of the field.
¹⁹ *By the sweat of your brow*
  you will eat your food
until you return to the ground,
  since from it you were taken;
for dust you are
  and to dust you will return."

²⁰ *Adam named his wife Eve, because she would become the mother of all the living.*

Note: There are just two curses—on the serpent and on the ground. The other descriptions by God are the natural result of going against what God had created and commanded—called "sin."

---

4. What do you think this creation story tells you about God?
   a. God can sure be tough when people screw up.
   b. God made everything and knows what's best.
   c. It's pretty hard to understand what God is up to.
   d. God did some amazing work before humans messed it up.
   e. Other _____

5. When you look at what the woman must experience (v. 36), what is the painful side of "Your desire will be toward your husband"?
   a. Husbands will take advantage of this attachment.
   b. I don't see a problem with it.
   c. The "desire" was meant to be toward God, and husbands aren't God.
   d. Power struggles replace partnerships.
   e. Other _____

6. For the man, work turns from rewarding into hard labor. Since most men no longer work with soil, what is the "ground" for men today that causes "painful toil"?

7. What thought from the Bible passages in this session tugs at your heart—something that makes you say, "Wow, I'd like to feel or know what that's like," or "Yuck, I'm glad that's not me"?

8. If you decided to believe that all humans are created with God's image (nature) inside, how might that affect your relationships with friends, spouse, people at work, people who are hard to like?
   a. I'd have to make some major changes in how I act.
   b. It really wouldn't make much difference.
   c. I don't want to consider it right now.
   d. I'd need help with my feelings.
   e. Other _____

ACCOUNTABLE COMMUNITY:

9. Is there a first step that you need to take this week that would improve one of your relationships?

   How can this group help you take that step?

WE SERVE:

10. What specific action will you take this week to help a person (between your house and the grocery store) know that they carry the "nature of God"?
    a. Make a 10-minute visit to a neighbor you've not talked to recently.
    b. Intentionally walk around your neighborhood and greet anyone you pass.
    c. Greet the store checkout person, asking how their day is going. Then thank them for their help.
    d. Other _____

WE PRAY:

Go around the group to share praises or prayer needs.

Ask for 1 or 2 volunteers to pray for specific items.

The group leader closes the meeting in prayer.

3: WHY DO PEOPLE ACT THAT WAY?

💡 THE BIG IDEA

In this story, we have a couple (Abram—later called Abraham; and Sarai—later called Sarah) whom God had promised would have a male child in their old age. We're talking old—about 100 years old. That child was to be the parent of a great nation. After being unable to get pregnant for a long time, Sarai decided to help God out and follow the tribal custom—giving her maid (slave) to Abram for sex in hopes that the maid would get pregnant—to become the surrogate mother.

This custom was not without its troubles, as wives and pregnant maids did not always get along well. There were many dynamics at play in these relationships. One was that women were primarily valued for their ability to birth and nurse children, particularly male children. You can imagine the clashes that would take place when a slave is seen as of "higher value" than her owner.

OPEN:

1. Think back to a time in your childhood when you were expecting a special gift, but didn't get it. What was it that you wanted so badly? Why do you think you didn't get it?

READ & APPLY: Genesis 16:1–16 (MSG)

1-2 Sarai, Abram's wife, hadn't yet produced a child. She had an Egyptian maid named Hagar. Sarai said to Abram, "God has not seen fit to let me have a child. Sleep with my maid. Maybe I can get a family from her." Abram agreed to do what Sarai said.

3-4 So Sarai, Abram's wife, took her Egyptian maid Hagar and gave her to her husband Abram as a wife. Abram had been living ten years in

Canaan when this took place. He slept with Hagar and she got pregnant. When Hagar learned she was pregnant, she looked down on her mistress.

⁵ Sarai told Abram, "It's all your fault that I'm suffering this abuse. I put my maid in bed with you and the minute she knows she's pregnant, she treats me like I'm nothing. May God decide which of us is right."

⁶ "You decide," said Abram. "Your maid is your business."

Sarai was abusive to Hagar and Hagar ran away.

⁷⁻⁸ An angel of God found her beside a spring in the desert; it was the spring on the road to Shur. He said, "Hagar, maid of Sarai, what are you doing here?"

She said, "I'm running away from Sarai my mistress."

⁹⁻¹² The angel of God said, "Go back to your mistress. Put up with her abuse." He continued, "I'm going to give you a big family, children past counting.

From this pregnancy, you'll get a son: Name him Ishmael;
  for God heard you, God answered you.
He'll be a bucking bronco of a man,
  a real fighter, fighting and being fought,
Always stirring up trouble,
  always at odds with his family."

¹³ She answered God by name, praying to the God who spoke to her, "You're the God who sees me!

"Yes! He saw me; and then I saw him!"

¹⁴ That's how that desert spring got named "God-Alive-Sees-Me Spring." That spring is still there, between Kadesh and Bered.

¹⁵⁻¹⁶ Hagar gave Abram a son. Abram named him Ishmael. Abram was eighty-six years old when Hagar gave him his son, Ishmael.

[Miraculously, later on, Sarai (Sarah) also got pregnant as God had promised and birthed a son named Isaac. The continuation of this story takes place at a time when the two boys were playing together, one day.]

Genesis 21:9–21 (MSG)

9-10 One day Sarah saw the son that Hagar the Egyptian had borne to Abraham, poking fun at her son Isaac. She told Abraham, "Get rid of this slave woman and her son. No child of this slave is going to share inheritance with my son Isaac!"

11-13 The matter gave great pain to Abraham—after all, Ishmael was his son. But God spoke to Abraham, "Don't feel badly about the boy and your maid. Do whatever Sarah tells you. Your descendants will come through Isaac. Regarding your maid's son, be assured that I'll also develop a great nation from him—he's your son, too."

14-16 Abraham got up early the next morning, got some food together and a canteen of water for Hagar, put them on her back and sent her away with the child. She wandered off into the desert of Beersheba. When the water was gone, she left the child under a shrub and went off, fifty yards or so. She said, "I can't watch my son die." As she sat, she broke into sobs.

17-18 Meanwhile, God heard the boy crying. The angel of God called from Heaven to Hagar, "What's wrong, Hagar? Don't be afraid. God has heard the boy and knows the fix he's in. Up now; go get the boy. Hold him tight. I'm going to make of him a great nation."

19 Just then God opened her eyes. She looked. She saw a well of water. She went to it and filled her canteen and gave the boy a long, cool drink.

20-21 God was on the boy's side as he grew up. He lived out in the desert and became a skilled archer. He lived in the Paran wilderness. And his mother got him a wife from Egypt.

2. As you look back over the story, what is the most frustrating part for you?
   a. Sarah's innability to get pregnant.
   b. Hagar's attitude toward Sarah.
   c. Sarah's abuse of Hagar, then kicking her out of the camp.
   d. Abraham's unwillingness to take charge of the situation.
   e. Hagar having to watch Ishmael suffer.
   f. Other _____

3. If you could drop into this tribal camp, which person's role would you WANT to take? Who would you NOT want to be? Why?

4. Why do you think Sarah made her own scheme instead of trusting God to help her get pregnant?
   a. God took much too long.
   b. She was an old woman.
   c. She wanted Abraham to love her.
   d. Abraham was getting impatient.
   e. Other _____

5. What common theme do you notice about how God shows up each time when Hagar is in trouble?
   a. God enters the scene at the very last moment.
   b. God waits until Hagar is desperate.
   c. The need is always met with abundance.
   d. Other _____

6. As you look at this complex story, what part of your own "story" is similar? How is your story different from the biblical story? Jot notes in the boxes, then discuss with your group.

Similarities:

Differences:

ACCOUNTABLE COMMUNITY:

7. What might be the greatest truth you could learn about God from studying this section of the Bible?

   _____
   _____
   _____
   _____

8. If you were to look deeply at your current life, which part reminds you of Hagar?

   Name the next step you need to take to get out of the situation? Whose help do you need?

WE SERVE:

9. Who do you know that is walking through a difficult situation, maybe just needing a friend to drop into their life? How can you "bless" that person this week?

WE PRAY:

Let the group list several items that they are celebrating this week:

Now make a list of circumstances that concern the group members:

The group leader will guide the group to first celebrate in prayer, then pray specifically for the group's concerns.

4: Who's Got Your Back?

💡 THE BIG IDEA

One of the key descriptors of God is that God is faithful—God is dependable and can be trusted.

The hero of this story is Joseph—a dreamer (he saw visions of the future) and an interpreter of dreams. Yet in his early life he was often obnoxious toward his brothers. He was also his father's favorite child, which made him envied and hated by them.

Young Joseph had a dream that he would one day become a great ruler over his brothers. And of course he told them about the dream, fueling their hatred even more. This hatred reventually boiled over and led Joseph's brothers to secretly sell him into slavery, to a caravan of traders headed for Egypt.

Once in Egypt, Joseph grew up and began to take responsiblity. He became the caretaker of a wealthy family's home. The homeowner's wife tried several times to seduce him, but when he refused she falsely accused Joseph of attempted rape and he was thrown into prison.

Joseph remained in prison for a long time until one day when the Egyptian ruler (Pharoah) had a disturbing dream and was told about Joseph's interpreting skills. After interpreting the Pharoah's dream—predicting a massive famine in the land— Joseph was released from prison and put into a leadership role to prepare for the coming disaster. In fact, he was made the second highest of all rulers in Egypt.

Through his trying ordeal, Joseph learned that God is faithful. In keeping a promise made to Joseph's ancestors, God elevated Joseph from the pit and later prison to the palace of Pharaoh where he could help save thousands of lives.

When the Egyptian famine arrived, it also hit Joseph's family back home in Israel. His brothers heard that Egypt had planned for the famine and actually had stores of food. During one of their trips to Egypt to buy food, they "bumped" into Joseph, whom they had sold into slavery many years earlier. Although he recognized them, they did not know him.

So Joseph took the opportunity to test his brothers several times, to see if they had changed from their vindictive ways when he was a boy. Finally, Joseph could keep the secret no longer and revealed himself to his brothers.

OPEN:

1. If you had $10,000,000 to help fulfill your wildest dream, what would you do with it?

READ AND APPLY: Genesis 45:1–19 (MSG)

1-2 Joseph couldn't hold himself in any longer, keeping up a front before all his attendants. He cried out, "Leave! Clear out—everyone leave!" So there was no one with Joseph when he identified himself to his brothers. But his sobbing was so violent that the Egyptians couldn't help but hear him. The news was soon reported to Pharaoh's palace.

3 Joseph spoke to his brothers: "I am Joseph. Is my father really still alive?" But his brothers couldn't say a word. They were speechless—they couldn't believe what they were hearing and seeing.

4-8 "Come closer to me," Joseph said to his brothers. They came closer. "I am Joseph your brother whom you sold into Egypt. But don't feel badly, don't blame yourselves for selling me. God was behind it. God sent me here ahead of you to save lives. There has been a famine in the land now for two years; the famine will continue for five more years—neither plowing nor harvesting. God sent me on ahead to pave the way and make sure there was a remnant in the land, to save your lives in an amazing act of deliverance. So you see, it wasn't you who sent me here but God. He set me in place as a father to Pharaoh, put me in charge of his personal affairs, and made me ruler of all Egypt.

⁹⁻¹¹ *"Hurry back to my father. Tell him, 'Your son Joseph says: I'm master of all of Egypt. Come as fast as you can and join me here. I'll give you a place to live in Goshen where you'll be close to me—you, your children, your grandchildren, your flocks, your herds, and anything else you can think of. I'll take care of you there completely. There are still five more years of famine ahead; I'll make sure all your needs are taken care of, you and everyone connected with you—you won't want for a thing.'*

¹²⁻¹³ *"Look at me. You can see for yourselves, and my brother Benjamin can see for himself, that it's me, my own mouth, telling you all this. Tell my father all about the high position I hold in Egypt, tell him everything you've seen here, but don't take all day—hurry up and get my father down here."*

¹⁴⁻¹⁵ *Then Joseph threw himself on his brother Benjamin's neck and wept, and Benjamin wept on his neck. He then kissed all his brothers and wept over them. Only then were his brothers able to talk with him.*

¹⁶ *The story was reported in Pharaoh's palace: "Joseph's brothers have come." It was good news to Pharaoh and all who worked with him.*

¹⁷⁻¹⁸ *Pharaoh said to Joseph, "Tell your brothers, 'This is the plan: Load up your pack animals; go to Canaan, get your father and your families and bring them back here. I'll settle you on the best land in Egypt—you'll live off the fat of the land.'*

¹⁹⁻²⁰ *"Also tell them this: 'Here's what I want you to do: Take wagons from Egypt to carry your little ones and your wives and load up your father and come back. Don't worry about having to leave things behind; the best in all of Egypt will be yours.'"*

2. As you've read the story of Joseph, what emotions have you been feeling inside? Make a line drawing below to show your "highs" and "lows." After a few minutes, show and describe your drawing to your group.

3. Think back to your own childhood. What story comes to mind that is similar to some part of Joseph's story? How is it similar?

4. After all that Joseph had been through from boyhood to manhood, how do you think he was able to forgive his brothers for what they had done?
   a. He realized that he had been a brat when younger.
   b. He had seen how God used the bad to bring about good.
   c. It was time to get on with life.
   d. They were still his blood-kin.
   e. Other _____

5 If you were one of Joseph's brothers, how would you have felt when Joseph revealed himself?
   a. Trusting—let bygones be bygones.
   b. Submissive—his dreams finally came true. Now we're his slaves.
   c. Panicked—let me out of here, quickly!

d. Cautious—let's see how this plays out.
   e. Other _____

6. From what Joseph says about God in this story, what could you say about God?
   a. God is a really cool dude.
   b. God is always working, even when I don't see it.
   c. God shouldn't let people go through all that bad stuff, first.
   d. God is dependable.
   e. Other _____

7. What do you think Joseph means when he says, "God sent me ahead to pave the way"?
   a. God used Joseph as a scapegoat.
   b. Joseph was part of God's plan to save others.
   c. God was Joseph's "dream maker."
   d. All this makes no sense to me.
   e. Other _____

8. If you were in a difficult situation and needed someone to help you get through it, on whom could you depend?
   a. A friend
   b. No one
   c. I have no idea
   d. A family member:
   e. Other _____

ACCOUNTABLE COMMUNITY:

9. Where do you need someone today to be dependable, to "have your back"?

How can this group help you this week?

How can this group best pray for you?

WE SERVE:

10. Who do you know that is having trouble getting a dream fulfilled? How could you help them take the first step toward their dream this week?

WE PRAY:

Ask for 2 or 3 volunteers to pray for the group's needs.

When the praying is completed, as a sign of agreement with the prayers, the group leader will guide the group to proclaim together:

"Because we agree with the prayers, together we say (or shout): **'Yes, let it be!'"**

5: Have I Gone Nuts?

💡 THE BIG IDEA

Disappointment, frustration, embarrassment, and anger ... we've all experienced those emotions. Our feelings get stepped on, a relationship fails, a dream shatters, a favor results in criticism instead of gratitude. And our news headlines describe the mayhem, pain, and death resulting from the actions of individuals who experience these emotions.

In this Bible story, David (one of the great, ancient Jewish kings) was a nomadic king-in-waiting; living in the countryside with his warrior band. Samuel the prophet had previously anointed him with oil (a Jewish tradition), and announced that he would be the next king. But the current king (an evil man named Saul) was still alive and frequently tried to kill David to keep him off the throne.

David had grown from the famous shepherd boy who fought the giant Goliath, into a popular "threat" to the king. Yet, when opportunity arose, David refused to fight or kill King Saul. Instead he hid in the mountains and counted on the locals to provide his food.

OPEN:
1. What is your most embarrassing or frustrating moment when you wanted to "lash out" at someone else? How did you act?

READ AND APPLY: 1 Samuel 25:1–34 (MSG)

[1] Samuel died. The whole country came to his funeral. Everyone grieved over his death, and he was buried in his hometown of Ramah. Meanwhile, David moved again, this time to the wilderness of Maon.

²⁻³ *There was a certain man in Maon who carried on his business in the region of Carmel. He was very prosperous—three thousand sheep and a thousand goats, and it was sheep-shearing time in Carmel. The man's name was Nabal (Fool), a Calebite, and his wife's name was Abigail. The woman was intelligent and good-looking, the man brutish and mean.*

⁴⁻⁸ *David, out in the backcountry, heard that Nabal was shearing his sheep and sent ten of his young men off with these instructions:* "Go to Carmel and approach Nabal. Greet him in my name, 'Peace! Life and peace to you. Peace to your household, peace to everyone here! I heard that it's sheep-shearing time. Here's the point: When your shepherds were camped near us we didn't take advantage of them. They didn't lose a thing all the time they were with us in Carmel. Ask your young men—they'll tell you. What I'm asking is that you be generous with my men—share the feast! Give whatever your heart tells you to your servants and to me, David your son.'"

⁹⁻¹¹ *David's young men went and delivered his message word for word to Nabal. Nabal tore into them,* "Who is this David? Who is this son of Jesse? The country is full of runaway servants these days. Do you think I'm going to take good bread and wine and meat freshly butchered for my sheepshearers and give it to men I've never laid eyes on? Who knows where they've come from?"

¹²⁻¹³ *David's men got out of there and went back and told David what he had said. David said,* "Strap on your swords!" *They all strapped on their swords, David and his men, and set out, four hundred of them. Two hundred stayed behind to guard the camp.*

¹⁴⁻¹⁷ *Meanwhile, one of the young shepherds told Abigail, Nabal's wife, what had happened:* "David sent messengers from the backcountry to salute our master, but he tore into them with insults. Yet these men treated us very well. They took nothing from us and didn't take advantage of us all the time we were in the fields. They formed a wall around us, protecting us day and night all the time we were out tending the sheep. Do something quickly because big trouble is ahead for our master and all of us. Nobody can talk to him. He's impossible—a real brute!"

¹⁸⁻¹⁹ *Abigail flew into action. She took two hundred loaves of bread, two skins of wine, five sheep dressed out and ready for cooking, a bushel of roasted grain, a hundred raisin cakes, and two hundred fig cakes, and she had it all loaded on some donkeys. Then she said to her young servants, "Go ahead and pave the way for me. I'm right behind you." But she said nothing to her husband Nabal.*

²⁰⁻²² *As she was riding her donkey, descending into a ravine, David and his men were descending from the other end, so they met there on the road. David had just said, "That sure was a waste, guarding everything this man had out in the wild so that nothing he had was lost—and now he rewards me with insults. A real slap in the face! May God do his worst to me if Nabal and every cur in his misbegotten brood aren't dead meat by morning!"*

²³⁻²⁵ *As soon as Abigail saw David, she got off her donkey and fell on her knees at his feet, her face to the ground in homage, saying,* "My master, let me take the blame! Let me speak to you. Listen to what I have to say. Don't dwell on what that brute Nabal did. He acts out the meaning of his name: Nabal, Fool. Foolishness oozes from him.

²⁵⁻²⁷ "I wasn't there when the young men my master sent arrived. I didn't see them. And now, my master, as God lives and as you live, God has kept you from this avenging murder—and may your enemies, all who seek my master's harm, end up like Nabal! Now take this gift that I, your servant girl, have brought to my master, and give it to the young men who follow in the steps of my master.

²⁸⁻²⁹ "Forgive my presumption! But God is at work in my master, developing a rule solid and dependable. My master fights God's battles! As long as you live no evil will stick to you.
   If anyone stands in your way,
     if anyone tries to get you out of the way,
   Know this: Your God-honored life is tightly bound
     in the bundle of God-protected life;
   But the lives of your enemies will be hurled aside
     as a stone is thrown from a sling.

30-31 "When GOD completes all the goodness he has promised my master and sets you up as prince over Israel, my master will not have this dead weight in his heart, the guilt of an avenging murder. And when GOD has worked things for good for my master, remember me."

32-34 And David said, "Blessed be GOD, the God of Israel. He sent you to meet me! And blessed be your good sense! Bless you for keeping me from murder and taking charge of looking out for me. A close call! As GOD lives, the God of Israel who kept me from hurting you, if you had not come as quickly as you did, stopping me in my tracks, by morning there would have been nothing left of Nabal but dead meat."

2. In their male-dominated culture, living with a "brutish" husband, what would you have told Abigail if she came to you for advice about visiting David?
   a. Are you nuts? We're all going to die.
   b. What will Nabal say?
   c. You're the only chance to save us.
   d. I'll go and die with you!
   e. Other _____

3. If you got the chance to be an actor in this story, which role would be the hardest to play? Why?

4. What was the main purpose for David to send his men to visit Nabal in the first place?
   a. Find out where the party was.
   b. Get some food for the troops.
   c. Tell Nabal how well they'd protected his shepherds.
   d. Other _____

5. Why do you think Nabal reacted so strongly against David's messengers?

6. How would you describe David's emotional state when he started down the trail with his warriors?
   a. He's a spoiled "hot-head."
   b. He's committed to bringing justice to a bad situation.
   c. He doesn't like being told "No."
   d. He's just plain out of control.
   e. Other _____

7. Note the carefully worded argument that Abigail presents to David. She was wise and courageous—taking her life in her own hands to stand up to a man.

   List at least 5 key points she makes:

   a. _____

   b. _____

   c. _____

   d. _____

   e. _____

8. When you find yourself frustrated or offended, are you more likely to respond like:
   a. the "early" David (act then think)
   b. the "later" David (cool off and be grateful you didn't act stupid)
   c. Abigail (a healer in a hot situation)
   d. Other _____

9. Abigail brought God's message to David, just at the right time, to keep him from committing murder. If you were to ask God for a just-in-time message in the middle of your frustration, anger, or feeling offended, what would you want to hear God say?

ACCOUNTABLE COMMUNITY:

10. What is your FIRST step in dealing with a specific frustration you face right now?

    How can this group help you take that next step, this week?

WE SERVE:

11. Who do you know that is going through a crisis that you could bring a good word to?

    What action will you take this week to serve them—to speak a word from God to them—and preserve their dignity while serving?

    _____

    _____

    _____

    _____

WE PRAY:

Group members *briefly* pray, either out loud or silently, for the person on their right.

6: Are You Kidding Me?

💡 THE BIG IDEA:

Many people have heard the Bible story about a man who was swallowed by a big fish (usually called a whale) and vomited up alive, three days later. That story is about a messenger of God (prophet) named Jonah. God had sent Jonah to proclaim the message of God's love to the people of a really evil city (Ninevah). The deal was that if they turned around to follow God, God would forgive them and they would not be destroyed.

But Jonah disagreed with God's plan to forgive the people of Nineveh. He wanted the people destroyed. He was so opposed to the plan that he boarded a ship headed in the opposite direction of Nineveh. When  the ship encountered a huge storm and nearly sank, Jonah ended up overboard—where he was kept from drowning by becoming the fish's lunch.

God got Jonah's attention. Jonah got God's message.

OPEN:
1. When did someone get a prize or award that you really wanted or thought you deserved. Where did it happen? A quiz show? At work? In your sports league?

   How did you feel toward the person who got the prize? Did you later interact with the person? If so, what did you want to say to them? What did you actually say?

READ AND APPLY: Jonah 3 (MSG)

1-2 Next, God spoke to Jonah a second time: "Up on your feet and on your way to the big city of Nineveh! Preach to them. They're in a bad way and I can't ignore it any longer." *3* This time Jonah started off straight for Nineveh, obeying God's orders to the letter.

Nineveh was a big city, very big—it took three days to walk across it. *4* Jonah entered the city, went one day's walk and preached, "In forty days Nineveh will be smashed."

5 The people of Nineveh listened, and trusted God. They proclaimed a citywide fast and dressed in burlap to show their repentance. Everyone did it—rich and poor, famous and obscure, leaders and followers.

6-9 When the message reached the king of Nineveh, he got up off his throne, threw down his royal robes, dressed in burlap, and sat down in the dirt. Then he issued a public proclamation throughout Nineveh, authorized by him and his leaders: "Not one drop of water, not one bite of food for man, woman, or animal, including your herds and flocks! Dress them all, both people and animals, in burlap, and send up a cry for help to God. Everyone must turn around, turn back from an evil life and the violent ways that stain their hands. Who knows? Maybe God will turn around and change his mind about us, quit being angry with us and let us live!"

10 God saw what they had done, that they had turned away from their evil lives. He did change his mind about them. What he said he would do to them he didn't do.

2. What do you think was going through Jonah's mind as he walked through the city on the first day?
    a. God, I'm doing what you told me, but I don't have to like it.
    b. Maybe I'll just speak really soft, so they won't hear me.
    c. I'm not going all the way in, so I can get out quick if they come after me.
    d. This place doesn't deserve forgiveness.
    e. Other _____

3. Why do you think Jonah only went a **third** of the way across the city, instead of **halfway**? Or across the whole city?

READ: Jonah 4 (MSG)

¹⁻² Jonah was furious. He lost his temper. He yelled at God, "God! I knew it—when I was back home, I knew this was going to happen! That's why I ran off to Tarshish! I knew you were sheer grace and mercy, not easily angered, rich in love, and ready at the drop of a hat to turn your plans of punishment into a program of forgiveness!

⁴God said, "What do you have to be angry about?"

⁵But Jonah just left. He went out of the city to the east and sat down in a sulk. He put together a makeshift shelter of leafy branches and sat there in the shade to see what would happen to the city.

⁶God arranged for a broad-leafed tree to spring up. It grew over Jonah to cool him off and get him out of his angry sulk. Jonah was pleased and enjoyed the shade. Life was looking up.

⁷⁻⁸But then God sent a worm. By dawn of the next day, the worm had bored into the shade tree and it withered away. The sun came up and God sent a hot, blistering wind from the east. The sun beat down on Jonah's head and he started to faint. He prayed to die: "I'm better off dead!"

⁹Then God said to Jonah, "What right do you have to get angry about this shade tree?"

Jonah said, "Plenty of right. It's made me angry enough to die!"

¹⁰⁻¹¹God said, "What's this? How is it that you can change your feelings from pleasure to anger overnight about a mere shade tree that you did nothing to get? You neither planted nor watered it. It grew up one night and died the next night. So, why can't I likewise change what I feel about Nineveh from anger to pleasure, this big city of more than 120,000 child-like people who don't yet know right from wrong, to say nothing of all the innocent animals?"

4. If you were walking along behind Jonah, taking notes during this whole encounter, what two questions would you have wanted to ask him?

   a. _____

   _____

   b. _____

   _____

5. What kind of relationship must Jonah have had with God to talk so bluntly?
   a. Jonah was a hard-head and didn't care.
   b. God was really patient.
   c. Jonah trusted that God would understand his emotions.
   d. Other _____

6. If you had the nerve, what really hard question would you like to ask God or complain to God about?

   What kind of response would you expect?

7. What is the most important new concept about God that you've picked up from this story?

8. When was the last time that you needed someone to come along and offer you a good word? A word of hope? A word of escape?

   Where in your life do you still need that good word?

ACCOUNTABLE COMMUNITY:

9. How do you need this group to help you move toward what you're beginning to understand about God?

WE SERVE:

10. What specific action will you take this week? As you are "out and about town," who might you offer a word of hope to?

_____

_____

_____

_____

WE PRAY:

Ask for concerns that the group should pray for. Then ask for a specific person to briefly pray for each item.

Dismiss when the last person has prayed.

7: How Will We Make It?

💡 THE BIG IDEA

There are times in life when we face too many crises, too much stress, too much pain, too much grief. This biblical story describes such a time for a woman named Naomi and her family.

In Naomi's culture, women were considered property of their men, and had no rights if they didn't have a husband or sons. As Naomi experienced the hopelessness of the worst of times she also discovered that she was not forgotten. The story is recorded in the Book of Ruth, the name of Naomi's daughter-in-law. Note the twists and turns, the emotional highs and lows of this wonderful story.

OPEN:
[Group Leader: If you have crayons or markers available, it will enrich the assignment.]

1. Remember back to a time, when you were 7–10 years old, when your family gathered for a special meal (or another occasion). In the space below, sketch the room, marking in all the people who were there. Use a symbol to identify each one. Then mark the person who was the magnet ... who held the family together. Share your picture with the group.

READ & APPLY: Ruth 1:1–22 (MSG)

1-2 Once upon a time—it was back in the days when judges led Israel—there was a famine in the land. A man from Bethlehem in Judah left home to live in the country of Moab, he and his wife and his two sons. The man's name was Elimelech; his wife's name was Naomi; his sons were named Mahlon and Kilion—all Ephrathites from Bethlehem in Judah. They all went to the country of Moab and settled there.

3-5 Elimelech died and Naomi was left, she and her two sons. The sons took Moabite wives; the name of the first was Orpah, the second Ruth. They lived there in Moab for the next ten years. But then the two brothers, Mahlon and Kilion, died. Now the woman was left without either her young men or her husband.

6-7 One day she got herself together, she and her two daughters-in-law, to leave the country of Moab and set out for home; she had heard that GOD had been pleased to visit his people and give them food. And so she started out from the place she had been living, she and her two daughters-in-law with her, on the road back to the land of Judah.

8-9 After a short while on the road, Naomi told her two daughters-in-law, "Go back. Go home and live with your mothers. And may GOD treat you as graciously as you treated your deceased husbands and me. May GOD give each of you a new home and a new husband!" She kissed them and they cried openly.

10 They said, "No, we're going on with you to your people."

11-13 But Naomi was firm: "Go back, my dear daughters. Why would you come with me? Do you suppose I still have sons in my womb who can become your future husbands? Go back, dear daughters—on your way, please! I'm too old to get a husband. Why, even if I said, 'There's still hope!' and this very night got a man and had sons, can you imagine being satisfied to wait until they were grown? Would you wait that long to get married again? No, dear daughters; this is a bitter pill for me to swallow—more bitter for me than for you. GOD has dealt me a hard blow."

14 Again they cried openly. Orpah kissed her mother-in-law good-bye; but Ruth embraced her and held on.

15 Naomi said, "Look, your sister-in-law is going back home to live with her own people and gods; go with her."

16-17 But Ruth said, "Don't force me to leave you; don't make me go home. Where you go, I go; and where you live, I'll live. Your people are my people, your God is my god; where you die, I'll die, and that's where I'll be buried, so help me GOD—not even death itself is going to come between us!"

18-19 When Naomi saw that Ruth had her heart set on going with her, she gave in. And so the two of them traveled on together to Bethlehem.
When they arrived in Bethlehem the whole town was soon buzzing: "Is this really our Naomi? And after all this time!"

20-21 But she said, "Don't call me Naomi; call me Bitter. The Strong One has dealt me a bitter blow. I left here full of life, and GOD has brought me back with nothing but the clothes on my back. Why would you call me Naomi? God certainly doesn't. The Strong One ruined me."

22 And so Naomi was back, and Ruth the foreigner with her, back from the country of Moab. They arrived in Bethlehem at the beginning of the barley harvest.

2. If your mother-in-law had been experiencing such pain-filled grief, what would you have said to comfort her?
   a. Suck it up and get on with your life.
   b. I'm so sorry that you're in such pain.
   c. I know just how you feel, and it's not really that bad.
   d. I'll stay here with you, until you're doing better.
   e. Other _____

[When Naomi and Ruth feared they would starve to death, Ruth volunteered to glean (gather grain) in the nearby fields. It was customary for the wealthy harvesters to leave a portion of the grain in the field for the poor to collect. So Ruth set off to gather in the field of a nearby landowner. After a few days ...]

Ruth 2:19–23 (MSG)

[19] *Naomi asked her, "So where did you glean today? Whose field? GOD bless whoever it was who took such good care of you!"*
Ruth told her mother-in-law, "The man with whom I worked today? His name is Boaz."

[20] *Naomi said to her daughter-in-law, "Why, GOD bless that man! GOD hasn't quite walked out on us after all! He still loves us, in bad times as well as good!"*
Naomi went on, "That man, Ruth, is one of our circle of covenant redeemers, a close relative of ours!"

[21] *Ruth the Moabitess said, "Well, listen to this: He also told me, 'Stick with my workers until my harvesting is finished.'"*

[22] *Naomi said to Ruth, "That's wonderful, dear daughter! Do that! You'll be safe in the company of his young women; no danger now of being raped in some stranger's field."*

[23] *So Ruth did it—she stuck close to Boaz's young women, gleaning in the fields daily until both the barley and wheat harvesting were finished. And she continued living with her mother-in-law.*

[Now the story takes a very strange twist. Naomi, concerned that Ruth would never remarry, sends Ruth to crash a party at Boaz' house. When he's had too much to drink, Ruth is to follow Boaz until he lies down to sleep. He ends up in the barn. When he's asleep, she follows the custom of her day, lying down at his feet, to show her availability for marriage. When Boaz awakens, he is startled to find her there—so Ruth confesses the whole story ... ending with how she and Boaz are actually distant relatives.

On the spot, Boaz commits to make marriage arrangements with Ruth, as is his responsibility, being a male relative (covenant redeemer). However, there is one person in the way, one other covenant redeemer with first rights to Ruth. But, by day's end, through intricate negotiations, Boaz is given all rights to Ruth.]

Ruth 4:13–17 (MSG)

¹³ Boaz married Ruth. She became his wife. Boaz slept with her. By GOD's gracious gift she conceived and had a son.

¹⁴⁻¹⁵ The town women said to Naomi, "Blessed be GOD! He didn't leave you without family to carry on your life. May this baby grow up to be famous in Israel! He'll make you young again! He'll take care of you in old age. And this daughter-in-law who has brought him into the world and loves you so much, why, she's worth more to you than seven sons!"

¹⁶ Naomi took the baby and held him in her arms, cuddling him, cooing over him, waiting on him hand and foot.

¹⁷ The neighborhood women started calling him "Naomi's baby boy!" But his real name was Obed. Obed was the father of Jesse, and Jesse the father of David.

[David was the hero king of Israel who wrote many of the Psalms in the Bible. We first met him in session 5.]

3. If this story were written into a movie, which person would you most likely cry for at the theater?
   a. Naomi, the grouchy mother-in-law
   b. One of the dead sons or father-in-law
   c. Ruth, the adventurous, try-it-all women
   d. Boaz, the caregiver
   e. Orpah, who stayed behind in Moab.
   f. Other _____

4. Who has "rights" to you? How do you feel about this?
   a. No one but me!
   b. My spouse and my children
   c. The bank!
   d. My employer
   e. Other _____

5. Following Boaz into a barn was risky for Ruth. How would you have responded if you'd been asked to participate in this crazy plan?
   a. I'd go anywhere and do anything to care for my loved ones.
   b. I'd tell Naomi that she was on her own!
   c. I'd look for "plan B."
   d. Sounds like a fun tradition.
   e. Other _____

6. Remember an experience when you stepped in to protect or provide help for someone in need.

   How did it feel? Would you do it again? Why or why not?

7. Ruth could have gone back to Moab; instead she followed Naomi into an uncertain future.

   When did you last face a time where you had to decide to turn back to what was familiar, or go forward into an uncertain future? What choice did you make?

ACCOUNTABLE COMMUNITY:

8. What is your "security policy" for your old age?
   a. My savings plan
   b. My IRA
   c. My children
   d. My wit and good looks
   e. I have no plan
   f. Trusting God to provide for me
   g. Other _____

9. Boaz was a good man who acted honorably and became part of God's plan—caring for Ruth and Naomi.

   How are you experiencing the reality of God caring for you in your life?
   a. I'm not experiencing it right now.
   b. I know God wants to make me different, but I'm not ready.
   c. I know how fortunate I am that God cares for me.
   d. I'm waiting for God to come through for me.
   e. Other _____

WE SERVE:

10. As a group, or as individuals, identify a family that has some practical needs you can meet. (Many local organizations will help make this happen; you may want to remain anonymous.)

    What will you do this week to be part of God's plan in a family's life?

WE PRAY:

Each person pray silently for the people they will serve this week. Ask God to use your efforts to truly help the person or people.

The group leader prays aloud to close.

8: Who Has the Map?

THE BIG IDEA

Moses is a great Bible and Jewish hero. But he wasn't always such a hero. Many people have seen a movie depiction of Moses leading the Jewish nation (Israel) across the divided Red Sea.

Yet, when he was born, Moses barely survived. In those days the Jews were living as a nation in Egypt. They had grown from one single family to many thousands of people. Feeling threatened by their sheer numbers, the Egyptian ruler (Pharaoh) ordered all male babies killed. To avoid losing her son, Moses' mother hid him in a basket-boat, in the river.

One day, Pharaoh's daughter came to bathe and saw the baby floating nearby. She decided to adopt him and save his life. Amazingly, Moses' mother was hired to nurse and care for him until he grew up and was moved to the palace.

When he grew up, Moses got caught in a set of circumstances that included killing one of the Egyptian masters (who was abusing a Jewish worker), and he had to flee for his life to the Sinai wilderness. In the wilderness he was taken in by a nomadic family and married one of the daughters. His career immediately switched from royalty to shepherding. That's where we find him in this story.

OPEN:
1. What is the most amazing invention that you have personally seen or used? (Technology, building, transportation, etc.) What "amazed" you about it?

READ AND APPLY: Exodus 3:1–12 (MSG)

1-2 Moses was shepherding the flock of Jethro, his father-in-law, the priest of Midian. He led the flock to the west end of the wilderness and came to the mountain of God, Horeb. The angel of GOD appeared to him in flames of fire blazing out of the middle of a bush. He looked. The bush was blazing away but it didn't burn up.

3 Moses said, "What's going on here? I can't believe this! Amazing! Why doesn't the bush burn up?"

4 GOD saw that he had stopped to look. God called to him from out of the bush, "Moses! Moses!"
He said, "Yes? I'm right here!"

5 God said, "Don't come any closer. Remove your sandals from your feet. You're standing on holy ground."

6 Then he said, "I am the God of your father: The God of Abraham, the God of Isaac, the God of Jacob."
Moses hid his face, afraid to look at God.

7-8 GOD said, "I've taken a good, long look at the affliction of my people in Egypt. I've heard their cries for deliverance from their slave masters; I know all about their pain. And now I have come down to help them, pry them loose from the grip of Egypt, get them out of that country and bring them to a good land with wide-open spaces, a land lush with milk and honey, the land of the Canaanite, the Hittite, the Amorite, the Perizzite, the Hivite, and the Jebusite.

9-10 "The Israelite cry for help has come to me, and I've seen for myself how cruelly they're being treated by the Egyptians. It's time for you to go back: I'm sending you to Pharaoh to bring my people, the People of Israel, out of Egypt."

11 Moses answered God, "But why me? What makes you think that I could ever go to Pharaoh and lead the children of Israel out of Egypt?"

¹² *"I'll be with you," God said. "And this will be the proof that I am the one who sent you: When you have brought my people out of Egypt, you will worship God right here at this very mountain."*

2. What do you think was the most difficult part of Moses' career change, from prince of Egypt to nomadic shepherd?
   a. The smell of the sheep.
   b. Missing the palace food and beds.
   c. Finding a meaningful role in life.
   d. All of the above.
   e. Other _____

3. Think about how you would respond if you came upon a talking, burning stop sign. What would you do?
   a. Walk away, pretending I'd not seen it.
   b. Stop to listen and see what was happening.
   c. Get some water and try to put out the fire.
   d. Ask another by-passer if they saw and heard what I saw.
   e. Other _____

4. Why do you think God needed to get Moses' attention in such a dramatic way?
   a. The desert noise was really loud.
   b. God wanted a dramatic entrance.
   c. The fire must have represented something special to Moses.
   d. Since the bush didn't burn up, Moses knew this was supernatural.
   e. Other _____

5. What impresses or surprises you about God choosing Moses for this mission?
   a. There must have been better leaders around.
   b. Moses had no proven track record.
   c. Moses was afraid.
   d. God believed Moses could do the job.
   e. Other _____

6. God's plan for Moses was huge. He left his shepherding to become the leader of a large nation, all because God told him to go. He was scared to death at the start, and many times along the way.

   If God showed up at your dinner table to give you a life mission/purpose, what would be the most frightening part?

7. Think about where your life is headed right now. If you could get a direct text or e-mail from God, what kind of purpose or mission would you hope God would give you?

   What would you want God to tell you?

ACCOUNTABLE COMMUNITY:

8. If you think that God has a purpose/mission for you, what is the next step you should take to get started in the direction toward fulfilling it?

   How can this group help you get started, this week?

WE SERVE:

9. How might you be "messenger from God" to someone this week? "Over-tipping" your restaurant server? Going out of your way to say "Hi" to a person sitting on a sidewalk bench? Intentionally greeting a neighbor walking by your house?

> Write your plan here:

PLANNING AHEAD:

Before you pray together, plan how you are going to wrap up this series of studies with a service event, a party, another outing, or all of the above. Set the date, place, and time. It doesn't have to be very formal. You may just gather at your normal group time but at a special location, with no agenda—just being together.

WE PRAY:

Now, form a huddle (if appropriate for your location) in the middle of the room. Give each person the opportunity to pray a brief prayer of THANKSGIVING for the person on their left. If anyone feels uncomfortable praying out loud, let them pray silently, ending their prayer with "Amen" so the next person knows it is their turn.

We Serve Together

Between group meetings, each group member is working to serve someplace in their community. IN ADDITION, the group should be dreaming of ways they can serve together, at least once while they are together in this study.

You probably, already know a great service agency in your area. If not, check out this short list of ideas to get you started.

One or two group members will need to take the assignment to research and contact the agreed-upon agency or agencies—to arrange the best time for serving. Then others can jump in to care for the details of travel to and from the site, covering meals, childcare, needed equipment, etc.

Let this time of service be a great event, and maybe the beginning of something more long-term.

Have a great time!!!

- **Most any community has an agency that serves homeless people.** You will need to research the options and the requirements for volunteers to serve. Look first for an agency that does more than serve meals, but that cares for the whole person. Certainly serving meals is important to those who are hungry, so don't discount those groups either.

- **Give Kids the World.** If you're not from Florida, this could be a group "workcation." Or you could help a family take their special needs child to GKW.

"The Village" is a 70-acre resort complete with over 140 villa accommodations, entertainment attractions, whimsical venues, and fun specifically designed for children with special needs. Located in Kissimmee, FL, Give Kids The World has welcomed more than 100,000 families from all 50 states and over 70 countries.

Give Kids The World can offer the perfect volunteering experience for church, civic, youth and many other types of groups. They provide a fulfilling and rewarding event for your group while accomplishing needed tasks and projects at their facility.
http://www.gktw.org

• **Look for an opportunity to work with the aging or homebound.** Many communities have agencies that you can partner with to serve this growing population group.

• **KaBOOM!** Do you know of a run-down playground or a place that really needs one? KaBOOM helps communities build playgrounds. They have contests to determine which communities receive the playgrounds and then look for volunteers to help build them. **http://kaboom.org**

• **Feeding America (formerly Second Harvest).** There are opportunities to help distribute food to those in need. Check out their website for the location nearest you.
http://feedingamerica.org

• **Habitat for Humanity.** You can help make a huge difference in a family's life by helping to build them a home. Habitat has a long history of great service and use of volunteers. Check out the website for the location nearest you. **http://habitat.org**

GROUP LEADER NOTES

TO GET YOU STARTED

FIRST!
It makes no difference whether you're guiding an administrative board, a sports-bar Bible study, or something in between. Every group needs to fundtion as a community of people who live in love with one another. So the following guidelines are adaptable to any setting.

WHAT IT'S NOT
These study sessions are NOT a place for you to teach the Bible to a group of people. The PRIMARY PURPOSE of these sessions is to create healthy relationships (with God and other humans) around scripture—to connect the "3 stories" (see "A Little Group Theory," below). People will learn the Bible as it makes real connection to their lives.

If you're an old pro at this small group stuff, we trust that the materials in this book will be a resource to help you move your group into a joyful and transparent community—to become a group of people who care deeply for one another and serve from that community—both to one another and to others outside the group.

AS THE LEADER
(the one who is responsible for getting the group together)
Your job is not to lecture, give advice, or anything else that sounds like teaching. You're the facilitator of this group of people.

HANG ONTO YOUR CHAIR
The idea of creating a small group may be a whole new (and scary) thought for you—especially a group outside the walls of your congregation. You may have been pushed into this role by someone who gives you a paycheck. Someone may have challenged you to a stretching experiment. Or you may have been wondering how to get your ministry to a deeper level. If any of those scenarios are true, just hang on and watch what can happen in the next few weeks.

GUIDE THE GROUP
As the team leader you will guide the group session (topic, time usage, etc.). Keep the group on track and within the time limits, even if each question is not answered or each activity completed. It is important to give time signals (at least 5 minutes and 2 minutes) when you must cutoff discussion. Every session must START and STOP on time. If some want to continue with discussion after the scheduled conclusion time, dismiss everyone and let those who want to stay, stay. This allows the group to respect those who must leave.

People will be energized for the next group session if they haven't felt trapped or been frustrated that they were just "killing time." Of course, you may hear some groans when time is cut short. Explain what you're doing—keeping your word to end the session on time. The complaining means that discussion was going well.

PLEASE ...
- Make sure that each person has a book or printout of the week's session. Everyone should have the same scripture version. IN FACT, ask people NOT to bring other biblical commentaries, books, etc., to the group, so everyone can stay focused on the specific Bible passage and questions. Commentaries

tend to shut down conversation because people believe they have the "correct answer" to questions.

- Respect each person for what they say, no matter how "off-base" it may seem.
- Set the time and place for the next group meeting.

- Care for group members and their families between meetings. That doesn't mean you do it all yourself. You encourage and coordinate (or have someone coordinate) the group members in their care of one another.

- Go FIRST in answering questions early on. It helps break the ice when you give an example of how you would answer a question.

- Break the group into 4s or 5s (try to never use 3s) for Bible study and the related questions. Then everyone will have a chance to contribute. Even the introverts who are nervous about speaking publicly will usually join in. Using 3s puts people into intimidating triangles.

- Carefully note "The Accountable Community" and "We Serve" sections near the end of each session. These are extremely important for the group life and ministry. Details are below.

A LITTLE GROUP THEORY

A. CONNECTING the THREE STORIES THROUGH GUIDED QUESTIONS

There are three stories that MUST connect if people are to discover what it means to be a whole person, and live in a vital, growing community. THE QUESTIONS are intentionally worded and placed where they are to help the THREE STORIES CONNECT around the Bible.

- The FIRST story is God's story (told through the Bible) that shows God's plan to create us as amazing humans, describes our walking away from God's plan, and explains God's becoming human to call us back home to wholeness.

- The second story is another person's life story, with all its stuff.

- The third story is "my" story, with all of "my" stuff.

When the three stories come together, amazing transformation happens.

- This model of small group is built on the fact that we need to tell our story, and connect that story to other people and to God.

- All of us have a child inside who wants to be released. These studies will help us "come to Jesus as a little child." So prepare to laugh and cry!

- CAUTIONS:
    1. We do NOT let people confess another person's "sins."
    2. People are only allowed to talk about their own issues.
    3. Gossip can kill a group. Often prayer requests are actually cloaked gossip. We must not allow people to talk about other people.
    4. Sometimes a person may dominate conversation with their own struggles—in a specific meeting or meeting after meeting. As a leader, you may need to talk directly to such a person, in private. A group cannot do therapy for an individual. That takes special care from a professional.

- As we tell our stories in the biblical context, the scriptures will become real to us. The goal of these studies is NOT to teach the Bible as a cognitive activity, just filling people's heads with memorized content.

- While some of the questions would seem needless if we're just trying to teach Bible, **they are important for building relationships**. And there is a specific sequence to the questions.

OPEN:
The **Open** question(s) is to get the group thinking about the biblical topic in a non-threatening way; often producing laughter, bringing out positive endorphins and reducing barriers to the deeper questions that are coming.

READ & APPLY:
The **Feeling** questions (those first 2 or 3 right after the Bible reading) are very important in helping people put themselves into the scripture passage.

The next **Scripture Content** questions are just that—questions to dig out some of the content. You may want to add more questions here, but do it carefully so you don't bog down the small group or lose sight of the overall purpose. The temptation is to try to "go deeper" in study, which usually means learning facts instead of allowing the Bible to transform our lives.

Many questions are given, but you are the leader and you should know your group. Since you KNOW THE PURPOSE (above) of the various questions, feel free to rewrite or adapt the questions for your needs. HOWEVER, as you adapt, keep the flow of questions going in the right order. You'll be glad you did.

THE ACCOUNTABLE COMMUNITY:
- **Personal Application** questions are where the scripture gets personal.

- **Community Accountability** pulls everything together with the group committing themselves to stand together for each person's personal growth and the group's health.

- During this time, you have the opportunity to guide the group in caring for one another.

WE SERVE:
Each session concludes with the opportunity for group members to serve in their community. This helps build a pattern of life for each group member and moves the group outside its own circle.

B. READING THE BIBLE

It's not unusual for people to be called on to read in a group. However, it can strike terror in any introvert or person with reading difficulties. Use these guidelines when preparing to read the Bible passages together as a group.

1. Unless you know a person really well, and their reading ability, never call on a person to read "cold turkey." This is especially true when reading the Bible, which may have difficult-to-pronounce words or complicated language structures.

2. The best way to prepare a person to read is pre-heating them before the session starts. Give them the opportunity to review the passage and plan for any difficult words or phrases.

3. If a person volunteers to read but then has difficulty getting through a passage, feel free to assist them by giving them a word or two and letting them attempt to continue.

4. Thank and compliment readers, particularly when the passage or pronunciations have been difficult.

C. A WORD ABOUT PRAYING TOGETHER

From session to session you will want to change the way the group PRAYS. Sometimes you'll want the group all together. Other weeks staying in the 4s will be best.

If you want to make your group members go "spitless" just ask them to pray out loud. But if you want to teach them to actually pray for one another, suggest various forms of prayer in a progressive way.

Level 1:
    After the group has shared concerns, you close by praying yourself.

Level 2:
    Ask for specific requests then ask for specific volunteers to pray for those requests.

Level 3:
    Ask two or three group members to volunteer to pray, then you conclude. Don't be afraid of silence for a moment or two.

Level 4:
    Ask the group to sit or stand in a circle and pray out loud around the circle by saying something like, "Dear God, this is _____. Thank you for _____. Amen."
    If anyone is uncomfortable with this plan, they can just say "Pass" when their turn comes.

You can also try variations of any of these, such as having the group pray silently around the circle for the person on their left.

Before long you'll have the whole group easily praying for one another. They just have to discover that it's safe to say what they're really thinking and feeling without the pressure to produce some form of "magic" words for God.

D. THE MISSION

Mission is vital to Christian growth. As a goal, each person should be serving someone else each week. The entire group should be serving together at least once each month. Of course, your group may not reach this goal right away.

However, as a leader, we can strongly encourage group members to complete the "We Serve" commitment between each session.

As for the group in mission together, see the "We Serve Together" section (p. 56) to help you get thinking about possible ways you can serve your neighborhood, city, and world.

In addition, the basic mission of the group comes in the form of an empty chair at each session. Each group member should constantly be on the lookout for friends and neighbors to fill the empty chair—to join your community of care.

It is important to plant the idea of MISSION or SERVICE at the very first gathering of the group. And continue to remind people of it each time the group meets.

E. BIRTHING NEW GROUPS

Much can be said about birthing new groups, but here are a few important guidelines.

Never use the term "split a group." Birthing is the healthy beginning of another group, out of an original group.

Once groups reach 10 to 12 people, the group needs to start planning the birth. However, "birthing" should be discussed at the very first group meeting, and every meeting thereafter, so no one is surprised.

Every group must have a group "Apprentice" as well as a "Leader." When birthing a new group, the original leader, with three to six people from the original group, leaves to start the new group. The apprentice stays to lead the original group. Both groups must then quickly find new apprentice leaders.

Birthing is easier if the original group and the newly-birthed group create a celebration party for the launch. You also might consider periodic "family reunion" parties for a couple of months.
Everyone is responsible for recruiting new group members to fill the vacancies created by the birth—and to grow the new-birthed group. Never forget the empty chair.

F. LAST BUT NOT LEAST

To be most effective in your ministry as a group leader, start seeing yourself as a pastor to your group. That's right, we said PASTOR.

Try saying that out loud to yourself:
"I am a pastor to this small group of people."

Congratulations, you did it!

You're not just a leader of meetings or the coordinator of some production. Your first role should be caring for the needs (particularly the Christian formation) of your group/team.

But before you reject the idea outright, think about it for a minute. Your congregation probably has another person whom you call "pastor." She or he oversees the larger ministry of the congregation. However, there is no way that one person can meet all of a congregation's many needs. The best care comes when a small group, led by its leader, takes responsibility for its team members. You are the "front-line pastor" to your "congregation."

This pastoring model may take the shape primarily of leading the small group sessions. But it should also include staying alert to the individual emotional, spiritual, etc., needs of your team members. In addition, it may mean hospital visitation or rallying the group for special support of a team member who is facing a crisis.

Here's another way to think of it: You are a COACH!

When you read that word COACH, your mind may race to individuals you've seen pace the sidelines of a court or field; some yelling, screaming and throwing things—others calmly watching and guiding the team.

But hundreds of years before the word COACH became a person, it was a vehicle. And that vehicle carried royalty—PRECIOUS CARGO.

Let that idea soak in your brain for a while.

Do we need to say it? When you are pastoring/coaching your group, you are carrying precious "cargo." You are helping God's Spirit move people from where they are right now to where God wants them to be, down the road.

But don't let that overwhelm you. This is God's ministry and we have the privilege of partnering with the Holy Spiri—who was at work long before you got to this place—and a team of people who can learn to care for one another.

So model care as you guide your group. Have fun watching what you and God can do together, to grow your group into a wonderfully caring community!

www.ingramcontent.com/pod-product-compliance
Lightning Source LLC
LaVergne TN
LVHW020100090426
835510LV00040B/2720